MW00931272

# Reading at ONE!

## A guide to early literacy exposure for toddlers and children

Naomi Bradley M.Ed

# DEDICATION

This book is dedicated to Jewell Murdock Hughes. I think of you often, rest well.

# CONTENTS

*Naomi Bradley M.Ed*

# ACKNOWLEDGMENTS

I cannot express enough thanks to my mother and husband for their continued love, support and encouragement. Faith and Michael Hill, Walter Bradley Jr., Love Grace, Charles Michael, and Faith Noel, I offer my sincere appreciation for believing in me, even in times when I doubted myself. You all are my inspiration.

My completion of this book could not have been accomplished without the unwavering support of my mother and father, Faith and Michael Hill. Thank you both for allowing me time to research and write. The countless times you have watched the babies during our hectic schedules will not be forgotten.

Finally to my caring, loving, supportive husband: Walter you have my deepest gratitude. There is no comfort that can compare with the relief I had in knowing that you were effortlessly managing our household activities while I completed my work. My most heartfelt thanks.

# CHAPTER ONE
## *WHO AM I?*

This all started back in 2009 when I began my teaching career at Hayes Elementary School in Kennesaw, GA. I remember that particular year there were a significant number of teacher layoffs in the state of Georgia. Teaching positions were both guarded and valued by those seeking them and those already employed. At Hayes Elementary that year there were four other student teachers, but I stuck out like a sore thumb because, I was the only black student teacher. Actually, I was the only black teacher in the entire primary school. The faculty was predominately white, the student makeup was predominately white, and then there was me; a bright eyed bushy tailed coed who knew very little about formal teaching.

The first couple of days we sat in large staff meetings, learning about the procedures of the school from the principal. The meetings had food and were entertaining to say the least. I felt like all the teachers were vying for attention. Teachers would do things like ask obvious questions, or tell stories that were completely irrelevant to the meeting focus. Some teachers even explicitly shout out an answer to a rhetorical question. One example of this foolery happened when we were in a meeting on differentiation. The principal asked the teachers to shout out some ways to differentiate instruction. (Differentiating instruction means to teach to different levels of learners and different learning styles.) Answers were shouting from everywhere in the room, the principal wrote the responses down. And as they started to dwindle from the crowd a teacher shouted out, "rigorous grouping". Now I was new to teaching at the time, but even I knew that she had just pulled that term out her butt simply looking for attention. How in the world do you group students rigorously? That just makes no sense at all. But se la vie…

It always puzzled me how teachers in meetings would do the very thing that they absolutely hated for students to do in the classroom. I.E. shouting out, talking while the presenter's talking, eating, etc. At any rate, my student teacher supervisor, the lovely L. C. would introduce me to all the staff whenever she past any teacher. I'll never forget one instance when L. C. introduced me to an older teacher who was obviously in her 29th or 30th year of teaching. To be honest, she was one of the few teachers who felt no resistance to my or any of the other student teachers being there. More than likely she saw no threat to our presence, realizing that her seniority gave her a job security unmatched in the building. We were sitting down at a long table eating a meal that the PTA provided; it was pulled pork sandwiches from a local restaurant, I believe. Well after pleasant introductions, the older teacher asked me, " Naomi, when is your last day with us?" I had absolutely no clue, so I wiped the barbeque sauce from my lip with a napkin, leaned back in my chair, and called out to another student teacher sitting a few seats away at the same table. For the sake of the story we can call her "Amy". I said, "Amy". I could see her look at me with her peripheral vision but she continued to ignore my calling her name. Finally, I was able to get the attention of the woman next to her, and said, " Can you get Amy for me". She did and when Amy leaned back from the table, she rolled her eyes and shouted, "What?" Her tone and body language towards me made everyone at the table take a second look at Amy. She must have felt all the eyes on her because she began to clean it up by faking a smile. After composing my emotions (I was furious), I responded, "Um do you know when our last day will be?" Unable to maintain the fakeness, she curtly responded, "I don't know, sometime in November." I returned to my conversation with the older teacher with no definite answer, but with a newfound realization about the public school system. Everything is a competition.

By no means am I ever one to shy away from talking about race. I mean perhaps Amy was a jerk to me because I am black. However, in my opinion, that particular encounter had nothing to do with race and everything to do with education. The disdain my cohort expressed towards me, I do not think was because I am black. It was rather because in her eyes I was her competition. As naïve as I was at the time, I hadn't viewed her in the same context. I never viewed her or any of the hired teachers as competition, because with all the teacher lay offs that year, I felt that the chances of me being hired were slim to none. You see at the end of our student teaching experience, in past years, there may be a teacher selected to be hired full time. I hadn't thought much about that being a reality. Therefore, I never thought I was competing. Oh, but how I was soon going to learn that everything in the public education system is a competition. Teachers compete against one another for teacher of the year, test scores, compliments from the principal, promotions, and the list goes on. Everything in public education is a big competition, but you see the downside to competition is that someone has to loose. In many instances the loser's in the competition have been the students. Why do I write this you ask? Well because while teachers and administrators are pointlessly competing against each other, students are suffering. Case in point, the Atlanta Public School cheating scandal of standardized tests. The driving force behind the teachers cheating, the principals allegedly asking them to, and the superintendent allegedly encouraging it, was invariably competition. Atlanta Public Schools wanted better test scores than the other metro Atlanta county school systems such as Fulton County, DeKalb County, Cobb County, etc. They wanted student improvement at any cost. Well the competition mentality that spurs the entire public education system had trickled down to me, and was staring me in the face. And well let's say the 21 year old me, was never one to shy away from a hardy competition. Therefore, I made up my mind that I would win.

During my student teaching I was often the first one through the door in the morning. I tried to make as many connections and impressions as possible with the other teachers. I wanted to soak up as much about teaching as I could from my supervising teacher L.C. There was even one instance where my kindergarteners were outside during a fire drill, and for some odd reason the principal was in the room. As we entered back into the building, for no reason at all about six kindergarten students decided that it was a good idea to run, dance and shout on the rug, after entering the building. I, having learned classroom management skills, told the students to "sit down crisscross applesauce" I then counted down from 5 to 1 and the students immediately stopped acting crazy and sat down on the rug. I could tell by the expression on the principal's face that he was impressed with how I handled the situation. On another occasion, during the reading block the principal came into the room and he had a visitor with him. I was reading a big book to the students and we were working on "Text to Self" connections. I would read a page or two and then ask the students a few questions for comprehension. I could tell by the look on both of their faces that they were very impressed with the instruction. Later, I found out that the visitor he had with him was actually the Cobb County superintendent! Well, to make a long story short by the grace of God, I was offered a teaching position at that school after my student teaching assignment was over. We were all outside during recess when the principal came outside and called me to the side. He offered me a position teaching first grade in the place of a woman who had gotten pregnant and was bedridden. I excitedly accepted and then proceeded to go to the bathroom (the kindergarten bathrooms were connected to the classroom). I went into the bathroom and shouted screamed and cried of excitement. I had done what was seemingly impossible at the time. I had landed a teaching job! However, the methods that drive my instructional practices and strategies that I will share in proceeding chapters of this book were taught in my four-month tenure as a teacher under the supervision of L.C.

During my student teaching, L.C and I would start every morning with what we eventually termed as "breakfast bunch". L.C. and another Kindergarten teacher from the classroom next door would bring coffee, donuts, and bagels and we would all sit in miniature chairs around a kindergarten size table and chat. Well to be honest, they would bring the treats, I was still in college and student teaching is not a paid position, so I would only bring breakfast every so often, when I could afford to contribute. The teachers were real sweet and understanding of the situation I was in. "Breakfast Brunch" may seem like an insignificant gathering to some, but it taught me a valuable lesson in time management. Time management is an integral part of teaching because our "breakfast bunch" would focus our day. There is a time to chat, and a time to teach, and a time to refrain from teaching. We rarely spent time talking about those things during the instructional day because we had already gotten most of our chatting out during "breakfast brunch".

Our instructional day would start off with "calendar math". L.C. would teach students the days of the week, months of the year, patterns, numbers, and money through repetition and song. (I will expand on those two topics in later chapters.) Every morning for about two weeks, I would watch L.C., stand in front of those kindergarteners and completely make a fool of herself; singing and dancing, chanting, and even cheering. I initially thought she was being foolish, but the students loved it, and they were learning. After about 1 week and a half L.C. handed her class over to me. When it was my turn to take over the class and begin my student teaching, I stepped right up and imitated L.C. as best I could. I sang, danced, chanted and even cheered. Although, I may have been making a complete fool of myself, the kids loved it, and they were learning! All of this was the baseline for the methods I used to teach my one-year-old daughter (20months) how to read.

# CHAPTER TWO

## *WHO IS LOVE?*

I never would have imagined that my first teaching experience would have impacted my life in such a profound way almost three years later, but it did!

Between the first time I student taught untill I birthed my first daughter, many things had transpired. I taught at three different schools, I married my college boyfriend, and I begun my masters degree.

It all started when I decided to change birth control pills. I wanted a new pill that I had seen on a television commercial with a lower dose of estrogen. I believed it would make me feel less sick. My husband and I were newlyweds and lets say less than "careful". Before I knew it my period was seriously late. After about two weeks of debating in my mind why I could be so late, I went to Family Dollar and picked up a pregnancy test.

This decision was made even after purchasing two different tests from the Dollar Tree and passing them both (meaning they indicted that I was not pregnant). For those of you who do not know the difference between the Dollar Tree and Family Dollar, let me explain. Everything and I mean everything, pregnancy test included are only $1.00 at the Dollar Tree; However, at Family Dollar things are sold at a discount price but, not quite as cheap as $1.00. My pregnancy test for instance cost about $5.00. Not to say dollar tree pregnancy test are ineffective, because there's a chance that I was taking them too early or perhaps the time of day I took them was the issue but at any rate the test I took from Family Dollar, at 5:30am the morning of March 8, 2012 was different and I was forced to accept the very thing I wanted, but wasn't quite prepared for. I WAS PREGNANT.

I slowly crept into the bedroom to tell my husband, who was half asleep. He was aware that I was taking the test and all the pregnancy talk we had been going through lately. Well, I proceeded to get dressed for work purposely not mentioning the results of the test. I wanted him to bring it up. After a few minutes he said, "So what did the test say? I replied, " It said I'm pregnant". He turned around facing away from me in the bed and pulled the covers over his head, like doing so would make the news change. I said well... "What should we do next?" A part of me was hoping he would say, "Let's go out and buy baby clothes!" but of course he didn't say that. My husband said, "I guess go to a doctor to find out for sure." I'm sure he was still very skeptical because I had passed two Dollar Tree pregnancy tests recently. At any rate a part of me was tremendously elated at the thought of being pregnant. I always wanted children. I always wanted to be a mother.

That same day that I took the pregnancy test, I went to work completely elated. Even the rambunctious and wild 5th graders I taught didn't get on my nerves that day. I could not wait to get off work and go to the doctor to get a more official confirmation of the pregnancy. The clock struck 3:10pm and I grabbed my purse and belongings and shot out the door of my job. I was off to my gynecologist office.

I arrived at the doctor's office a little before 3:45pm and attempted to check in. The lady at the desk had curly red hair, and she looked to be in her middle to late forties with freckles and large brown-rimmed glasses. She looked like she couldn't be more ready to get off from work, go home and feed her cats. She proceeded to ask if I had an appointment while I signed in on the clipboard. I said nervously, "Well ... no I just needed to get a pregnancy test". She said very frankly, "I can make you an appointment for Monday at 4:00pm, because we don't take walk in's". I looked around at a completely empty waiting room and office, unable to believe my ears! Seriously? One simple pregnancy test couldn't be given until Monday!!! It was Thursday! I needed to know today. Shoot I needed to know yesterday! or two weeks ago for that matter. I politely took the appointment card she gave and asked her if she knew of any doctors offices that did take walk in appointments. With reluctance in her voice she told me about a clinic about a block away.

I departed from the office in a bit of a rush; scared that the clinic would be closed soon. It was approaching the end of normal business hours at 5:00. I arrived at the clinic at 4: pm and checked in. While sitting in the waiting room I noticed the hours of operation sign on the wall. It stated office hours are 6:00am-9:00pm, so I could relax knowing that I had plenty of time. The receptionist was a very nice, brown skinned woman with a round face. She took my insurance card and asked if I had a deductible. I was very confused by her question. At that point I was only familiar with the term deductible in reference to cars. I wondered, why was this woman asking me about my health insurance having a deductible? I honestly told the receptionist that I don't know. She said, "All right honey I can look it up and find out". I know she must have been thinking, "What an idiot to not know what kind of insurance you have". She would be right in thinking that, I should have been a lot more aware of the coverage I selected.

Soon after I checked in at the front office, I was called in the back room for the normal practices done at medical facilities. The nurse took my heart rate and blood pressure and began asking me questions. She asked, "Have you been having any symptoms of pregnancy?" "Why do you think you're pregnant?" She rattled off a number of symptoms and I tried to make myself believe as though I had actually been experiencing those things although I hadn't. At that point in my pregnancy I was feeling fine. Actually I was feeling so fine that I questioned if I was even pregnant myself due to my lack of symptoms. I found out much later how everyone's pregnancy is different. As much as people want to lump all pregnancy symptoms together and tell you how you should feel, it just differs for each individual person.

The nurse spoke to me briefly, then handed me a plastic cup and directed me to the bathroom. I peed in the cup as directed and then was led to sit in a tiny room to wait for the doctor to come in and share with me the results. I really felt like it took forever for him to come. I tried to not play with my phone because I think that's tremendously unprofessional in a place of service. All kinds of thoughts ran through my mind while waiting for the doctor. "Am I really pregnant?" "I just got married 4 months ago!" "What do I do next if I am pregnant?" "How will my husband really feel about this?" Just as I was about to let all these thoughts get the best of me the doctor finally walked into the room.

He was a tall black man. He was an older guy with salt and pepper hair on his head and on his face with kind eyes. He greeted me, and looked at his clipboard and said, "Well Mrs.

Bradley congratulations you are indeed pregnant." I felt like time stood still as he spoke. All the uncertainty of the moment's prior fell and as the teenagers say these days, "it got real"! He pulled out a circular cardboard wheel and asked me, "Well when was your last period?" I told him it was January 15, 2012. He twirled the wheel, adjusted his glasses, then said, "You are about 7 or 8 weeks pregnant, so your expected due date is between October 1-20." I tried to write the information down on a little notepad I had in my purse as quickly as I could. The moment he said the due date really struck me, because if nothing else made that moment real, knowing that I had a due date solidified it for me. I was really pregnant and it was even doctor confirmed.

At that point in my consciousness, I, like most people didn't believe anything unless a medical doctor said it. When the truth is that a doctor is only an instrument through which God works. Just as God works in each one of us; doctor or not. Whether the doctor confirmed my pregnancy or not the work of The Lord was being done well before the doctor spoke and well after the doctor spoke and not a result of the doctor.

The doctor said he would write me a prescription for prenatal vitamins and I could check out with the receptionist. He also said he would bring the prescription out to me with a list of possible obstetricians to consider.

I went to the counter where the receptionist had my insurance card. She looked worried and said, " You have a deductible". There goes that word deductible again I thought. I said, " So how much do I owe you, a million dollars?" jokingly. She smiled and said, "wait a minute" and she proceeded to call over my doctor. She tried to explain to him what was going on with my insurance. I could tell by the tone of the conversation, they were discussing how the paper work could be manipulated in the system for me to pay less. After trying a few options they concluded that nothing could be done and I was charged $165.00 for the visit. Well that was quite a stretch from the normal $10.00-$20.00 copay I was used to paying while under my mothers insurance. I was so elated at the news of being pregnant that I did not think much about the price. I simply pulled out my debit card, paid it and went to a pharmacy to get my prescription filled. I felt so blessed that I WAS PREGNANT! Little did I know what changes for my life that meant.

So, needless to say in my one bedroom apartment, I may have been the only one extremely excited about the pregnancy news. Upon a suggestion from my mother I purchased some sparkling grape juice and celebrated! Even if by default I had to celebrate alone. The truth is, I was very happy regardless of whether we had any money or the fact that my husband was only working part time, or that my 2nd year teaching salary fell just short of us qualifying for government assistance programs. I knew that the life that growing inside of me was a blessing regardless of any outward circumstance. So I drank my bottle of sparkling juice and toasted myself to the fact that in about 7 months I'd be someone's mother!

My husband didn't seem too excited. From what I hear most men aren't. So he said little to nothing to me about the pregnancy or the baby. However, I did discover through snooping through his text messages that he was telling all his buddies about his excitement and joy of being an expectant father. Why he choose to keep his excitement from me was something I could not understand. He was in his own way happy and excited I guess.

Several women believe that pregnancy news is a magical moment for the husband and well to some, it may be. However, men are different from women in many ways and I know all my husband could really think about at the time was probably finances or lack there of. I knew my husband eventually wanted children, but to have children come up so early in our marriage may have been too much for him at the time. I do commend him for not being a jerk about the situation we both faced. He was just quiet about it a lot.

I spent the next few days figuring out what doctor I would receive medical care from, and in doing so I received some life changing news. I had told a few of my coworkers about the pregnancy and they informed me that I needed to also, elect short term disability to pay for the days I would miss work on maternity leave. I didn't like the idea of being considered disabled from having a baby but if it would give me some money while I'm not working I figured, why not give it a shot.

I learned that short-term disability is only offered through my employer, so I called the benefits department. The benefits department informed me that I missed open enrollment and also missed the deadline to request short-term disability due to a life-changing event i.e. my wedding. I researched and called every outside company in the phone book for short-term disability, only to discover that no one would cover me because apparently pregnancy is a pre-existing condition, not covered under short-term disability. So here was my first predicament. I would eventually have to take about 6 weeks off from work that I would not be paid for. That of course was provided there were no complications, which would prolong my time off. Not to mention that I had very little sick days to put towards my maternity leave, because I had only been teaching for two years, and hadn't accumulated many days. I had to come up with at least $3,000 to supplement the funds that would be gone when I'm not working. Well, on the bright side, at least I had insurance, so having the baby would be easy on the pocketbook, or so I thought.

I decided to call a doctor that worked at an office and delivered at a hospital not too far from our apartment. While pregnant, the question you will find that other women ask you a lot is "where are you having your baby?" I think in this day and age it has become a huge status symbol associated with where you deliver. Everyone in the Atlanta area wants to go to Northside Hospital or Emory Hospital. They like to talk about how the staff is so nice there and how they give you gift bags when you leave blah blah blah. In a sense, you can be made to feel by others that not having your baby at the right hospital is doing you and your child a disservice. I mean who wouldn't want a gift bag?

One day while my fifth grade students were at Physical Education class, I used my planning period to call the doctors' office. The receptionist first asked for my insurance information, my group number, street address, social security number, etc. I provided my insurance number and she said, "per your deductible you will have to pay $298 for your first prenatal doctors' visit". I did not understand. Why would a doctors' visit be so expensive? I inquired about why my insurance wouldn't cover the visit. She frankly replied, "You have a $1,500 deductible. I was even more confused and beginning to get upset, so she told me to check with my insurance company and have them explain my benefits. I hung up the phone and immediately called my insurance company. After minutes, which felt like hours of being on hold I was finally able to speak with someone about my insurance. She told me that I had a "high deductible plan". According to my plan, I had to pay $1,500 out of pocket before my insurance would cover $3,000 of medical expenses. I could not get my mind wrapped around $1,500. Where in the world would that money come from? At first, I became defensive. I told her there is no way I would elect such a plan and there must be a mistake. I became overwhelmed with sadness knowing that I did in fact elect that plan. At that moment of sadness, one of my students walked in the room having forgot her inhaler for P.E., I quickly turned my head away from my desk to hide the tears running down my face.

You see, I was single at the time of enrollment of health insurance and actually very healthy for my age. Therefore, I never put much thought into selecting a coverage plan. I would just pick the least expensive plan. The previous year, I was still under my mother's coverage for health insurance and without thinking about the possibility of becoming pregnant this year, I selected the cheapest health insurance available. "What a mess I've put myself into I thought as I continued to sob uncontrollably." All

I could think about was that I wouldn't be able to even afford having my baby. The health insurance lady on the line could hear my crying and began asking questions sympathetically. She asked, "oh sweetie what's wrong? Why are you so upset? Are you having a medical problem?" I told her that I was 7 or 8 weeks pregnant, and she replied surely out of reflex, "Oh NO!" Her response is pretty funny now that I've sorted my situation out, but at the time I felt like even she knew what kind of predicament I was in having selected a high deductible plan. After doing my research thoroughly I found out exactly why she replied "Oh No". Absolutely no doctor would deliver a baby for less than $7,000 and that was not including prenatal care and doctor visits. I was essentially up the creek without a paddle. Even if I could some how find $1,500 dollars and the insurance company would cover $3,000, I would owe about $4,000 of medical expenses that I would have to provide. This meant that on my end I would have to come up with roughly $5,500 just to have my baby. Not to mention the baby's hospital cost. I cried and cried not knowing where that kind of money would come from.

I called my mom pretty much hysterical about the news and she couldn't believe that a plan like that would even be offered to a woman of childbearing age. Her astonishment of my predicament did very little to comfort me. I still cried and cried on the phone to her about the situation. Finally having had enough of my sobbing, I suppose, decided it was time to put things back into perspective before I started becoming too depressed. She asked a question which she asked quite often when she found me in need of a reality check. She asked, "Who's in charge?" Through tears I replied, "God is". She said "That's right, so you know that God is not going to give you anything you can't handle, just know it will all work out." I was hoping my mom would say, oh honey here's a magical pot of money I found so you can have to have your baby, but she didn't say that and knowing she lived on a fixed income she couldn't say that. I said, "ok" and we hung up the phone and ended the conversation. After talking to my mom I felt much better about it all. I went to the bathroom and washed my face. I knew I had to stop crying because nothing is worse than a crying teacher. Fifth graders can seriously smell fear and any signs of weakness.

The moment I finally was able to pull myself together, I started down the hallway to share the news with my coworkers. In this particular situation, I had to laugh to keep from crying and one of my male coworkers said, "Well what are you going to do?" I said I guess I'm going to just have my baby at home," jokingly of course. He said adamantly, "Oh no there is no way you're doing that!" He handed me a dollar out of his wallet, he said this is towards your hospital fund. I said, "thank you" and we all had a huge laugh about it. Having a baby at home was such a crazy idea to us all that we had a good hearty laugh about the notion. Little did I know that having a home birth was ultimately going to be my best option.

In playing with my coworkers I began to lookup home births on my laptop whenever my coworkers were around. This was just to get a rise or either a laugh out of them. But, something happened while I began looking up pages to joke with them about. I began looking at these women in pools and at home giving birth. I began reading they're stories and became infatuated; even obsessed. Every testimony I read about home births was more beautiful than the last. I learned about midwives and doulas and the role they played in the home birthing experience. I loved all the information I researched and finally came to the conclusion that I would indeed have a home birth.

The information that I found on the Internet forced me to research my own family history. I started with my mother. She naturally gave birth to three babies. By natural I mean she had no epidural, and no C-sections, no medication at all. I also found out that my father was a product of a home birth, meaning his mother, my grandmother delivered naturally at home with a midwife twice. Once with him and his older brother in Milledgeville, GA. Knowing the history of natural childbirth in my own family brought great comfort and empowerment to the decision I made. Becoming aware of my own family history of home and natural births made the decision seem less strange and uncommon.

I remember the first time I broke the news to my husband. A part of me did not know what kind of reaction I would get. Would he feel like the idea was too out of the box? Would he completely not want a home birth at all? Would I have to show him the research I have found about home births? Would the research even matter to him? Well all the things I thought he would say he didn't. He said very honestly, "Whatever you decide I will be behind you 100%." That was a huge weight lifted off of my shoulders, knowing that I had his support with the decision. He said, "Even if you decide to give birth in a car I'm okay with that too, whatever you choose." It was such a blessing to know that we were on the same page with how our first child would enter the world.

Around the time we discussed having a home birth my

husband had convinced himself that he had high blood pressure. He had been testing his blood pressure on the machines they have at the pharmacy of Wal-Mart and other drug stores. I believed he had hypertension because things were moving so fast for us. Within about 14 months he had proposed. We had gotten married and had a baby on the way. Not to mention that, we were beginning the process of purchasing our first house. All of that going on was surely enough stress to raise his blood pressure. Not to mention my sometimes-erratic mood swings were probably no stress reliever at the time. So after weeks of exercise and other measures he still couldn't get his blood pressure down to a normal range. At the time my husband didn't have any health insurance. He was only working a part time job( this was before Obamacare), so I suggested that he go see a natural-path physician I heard about from church named Dr. Mark.

I always was and am a firm believer that natural measures should be tried before fully and whole-heartedly trusting the medications of clinical physicians. My husband had his appointment made for about two weeks out and in those two weeks I was on a bit of a mission to find good a midwife to deliver my baby. I called reputable physicians and tried to get references on a midwife. I even asked the school nurse where I worked if she knew of a good midwife. My search came up seemingly empty at every corner. Then one day it hit me to ask my husband to ask Dr. Mark for a referral.

Now my husband has an incredible "gift" for conveniently missing or not hearing request I have of him. However, this appeal of asking Dr. Mark for a midwife referral I could not have ignored. I needed him to ask Dr. Mark if he had any references for midwives while at his appointment. I continued to remind him daily and even reminded him the day he went to see Dr. Mark. That night when he came home he had the name and number of a midwife that Dr. Mark pretty much told him was the best in the business. I was so grateful that my husband remembered to ask and even more grateful that Dr. Mark was able to give a referral.

"Her name is Nasarah, and Dr. Mark said that she is an awesome midwife". With a reference like that from Dr. Mark I figured I'd better give her a call, so I did. I picked up my cell phone, looked at the little piece of paper her number was written on, and decided to give her a ring. "I really wished this woman had an email address, or a website link, or a Facebook page," I thought as I looked at her number about to call. I'm a full product of the technology generation. I think in a sense having so many different ways to communicate inhibits the genuineness and simplicity of talking to an actual person at times. I'd much rather email, or text someone I don't know rather than call them on the phone. This sounds crazy to most people but ask anyone under the age of 27 and I'm sure they would share my sentiments.

At any rate, I knew finding a midwife was not going to happen on its own, so I hesitantly dialed her number. The first time I called, the phone rang and rang until her voicemail answered, which I found to be a huge relief. I wouldn't actually have to talk that much. I could just explain my situation briefly and wait on her to respond. She called back about ten minutes later. She said in a voice that sounded very sweet and older, "Greetings, did someone just call Nasarah". "Dang," I thought. This question proves that she didn't listen to my message and I would have to explain myself all over again. "Why did she say greetings instead of hello? That's different", I thought. I cleared my throat and said, "yes, my name is Naomi Bradley and I am pregnant and would like to know your rates for your midwife services." She said in a soft, kind, grandmotherly voice, "Oh you're pregnant that's wonderful, How many weeks are you? And how did you find out about me?" I told her about my husband and Dr. Mark and she interrupted, "Oh I just LOVE Dr. Mark, isn't he wonderful? I said, "yes" he is even though I had never even met the man. He had only met my husband.

On the phone she was so warm and familiar that I had to

remind myself to stay focused on the task at hand, which was to get a rate quote for services. At this point that was the most important thing, because my most recent encounter with the medical field essentially came down to money. I have even heard of women being billed months before they even deliver! Because of this, I asked her a few times, how much do you charge? She told me the amount for the initial consultation and that all other fees would be discussed after we met face to face. She said wait a minute while I check my appointment book. I could hear the pages rustling in the background and thought, "Hmm she must be an older women to have an appointment book and not have all appointments scheduled on her phone or on a computer". She gave me some options and we settled on a date and time.

Before we hung up she asked me to keep a food diary of all that I ate everyday up until the appointment. She also emphasized the importance of drinking plenty of water. I could sense from our conversation that she was a very genuine and caring woman. Her nonchalant-ness about fees and concern for my diet were a huge comfort. It was a complete contrast from conversations held with doctor's. I felt that they didn't care much at all for my well being. They just wanted to me to know how much services were going to cost and if I was prepared to pay them period. I left the conversation with Nasarah very grateful that I was forced to call and actually talk to her. It gave me much more assurance than any email ever would have.


Our appointment was set for a Saturday morning at 10:00 am at one of her doula's home. A doula is a woman who assists during the childbirth providing the mother with everything that she needs and everything the midwife needs. Coincidentally my husband and I arrived at the home at the same time as the midwife. As soon as I saw her, I knew that she was the person I'd been looking for and didn't even know it. She had smooth, deep brown skin like my husband. She couldn't be more than 5 feet tall. She wore a hat but her long wavy hair was visible out of the hat with sprinkled strands of grey interwoven in the four or five platted braids. A floral printed skirt flowed over her curvy body and a bright warm smile illuminated her face as she gave my husband and I a big hug.

We entered the living room of the doula's home after we took off our shoes of course. My husband and I sat together on a full couch while Nasarah sat cattycorner to us in a rolling chair and the doula sat on the floor in front of us. I could tell my husband was very curious because he kept looking around at the things in the house without having too much input into the conversation. Just doing as he normally does, looking, and listening.

We all sat there for about a minute enjoying a silence that was neither awkward nor uncomfortable. I guess we were just embracing one another's energy. Nasarah began the conversation by asking me what made me decide to have a home birth. After explaining my story we discussed any questions my husband and I may have had. Something that struck me immediately was when I asked about the pain of birth. I was immediately interrupted by

Nasarah who told me, "There is no pain, and we don't even use the word pain because the birthing experience is not painful. "What? I thought to myself I have NEVER heard that before, every woman I've ever talked to has spoken about how painful it was. I wondered, "Is this midwife trying to use some kind of Jedi mind trick on me? "Later I would find out exactly what she meant about no pain. Her doula interjected saying that giving birth is an out of body experience, where the mother, during labor actually leaves her body and travels to another realm in order to retrieve the spirit of the child and return with it. "Hmmm" I thought. I had never heard of childbirth told quite like that.

Nasarah asked if we had any questions and of course I had plenty. I asked what would she do if the child was breach? She described the method she used and how simple and often breach babies occur. I asked about every possible complication I could think of as she told me there's no such thing as complications only healthy births. The doula interrupted her then to tell me a story about how her mother swears by Nasarah. She said with her third child her uterus came out with the baby upside down, Then Nasarah, without skipping a beat, simply prayed a prayer, and placed the uterus back inside her. After that Nasarah successfully delivered two more of the woman's children.

This story to me was not only a testament to the effectiveness of the midwife but so much to me a confirmation that she was the answer to the question posed to me by my mother days ago about who was actually in charge. I wanted someone to assist in bringing my child into the world. Someone who was competent and as aware as I was that no matter what, God is in charge. Nasarah was that woman; we had found our midwife.

# CHAPTER THREE

## *WHAT THIS BOOK WILL TEACH*

My daughter, Love was delivered by the best midwife in Georgia. She is the product of a planned homebirth. She came out screaming like a banshee and she hasn't stopped, just kidding. When she was born I had a mere 6 weeks to bond with her, before having to return to the classroom and teach. I took full advantage of those 6 weeks by learning my baby. Many mothers' especially new mothers spend countless hours reading about their baby and not much time at all reading their baby. By "reading your baby" I simply mean observing, interacting, and listening to the child. For example, Love like most babies was always enamored with lights. She would stare and smile at lights, mirrors, and Television. She turned to light no matter how we would try to redirect her attention. I will focus on TV in a later chapter so don't worry. I found that Love was speaking to me through the attention she was showing to lights and sounds. She was telling me that she is a visual learner. Although people have multiple intelligences and learning styles such as musical, linguistic, artistic, active, etc. babies often demonstrate their preference very early on. You have to listen to your baby.

When I returned to work my mother took excellent care of my baby Love. Although, I had the best teacher and caretaker in the world watching her, I thought about my baby constantly. As a result of this, I would take every opportunity possible to hear her voice. I would call on my lunch breaks and planning periods, and I constantly looked at pictures of her on my phone. Like most mothers I thought my baby was flat out smart! So I was always looking to give her the best educational start. One day I decided to make Love some flashcards. The reason I made her cards instead of simply buying them is because often times the phonemes (the way letters sound) and graphemes (the way letters are written) conflict greatly with store bought cards. For instance the flash card may read the letter "E" then show the word with the picture "eye". This is completely wrong, so instead of spending time correcting mistakes, I chose to simply make my own cards, which I knew would have the accurate parallels between the letters and sounds. After I created and printed the cards a few of my students who stayed after school, colored them, and then I laminated them. Everyday when I went to my mother's house to pick Love up, I would go over the letter flash cards with her and she loved it! (The specific methods I used in reviewing the flashcards will be explained in a later chapter). There was a point when I would walk through the door and Love would hand me the flashcards, and my mother would say, " you know she already made me read those three times today!"

I know you are reading this saying to yourself, "That's

exactly what my Michael, or my Emory does!" Well that is the point of this chapter on Love. Love, as special and exceptional as she is in my eyes is no different from your baby on a very simplistic level. "Love" is everyone's child. Love is little Michael and little Emory. Love could read at the age of one because of deliberate instruction and communication with her. Exactly how this was done will be shared in detail as we delve further into the book.

## *Everything is Everything*

## *(The subconscious mind of your child)*

# CHAPTER FOUR

## *MUSIC*

Most parents are aware that children are always listening, especially when you think they are not. Well that fact reins true of babies and toddlers. When my daughter, Love was in the womb I remember putting plugs of classical music to my stomach. I also sang to her while she was proverbially, "baking in the oven". This set the stage for brain stimulation. In order for authentic learning to occur the brain must be stimulated. Now if your child is already born and you are thinking that you have dropped the ball by not singing to the baby and playing music, do not worry, as there are other methods that can be used to stimulate brain development through direct instruction. For example, Love was always a "pistol starter". As a baby, she would cry and yell and scream to her wits end. To calm her down in my absence, my mom would sing to her. As corny as it sounds, my mom would sing "Love lifted Me" (A play on her name "Love") and each and every time my mom would sing, Love would calm herself. One particular time Love, my mom and I were traveling to run errands and Love was wailing her head off in the car. One tactic I would use when this would happen is to turn the radio on full blast to drown out the crying. My mother turned down the radio, and began singing; "Love lifted me" Within seconds Love stopped crying. She was quieted by the voice of my mother singing. The only drawback was that Love would immediately return to wailing after the song was over, thus forcing my mother to sing to her the entire car ride.

It has been said that when you sing to your baby, it is like taking them to college. The brain stimulation initiated through singing is and has been unarguably the easiest and most significant thing you can do to give your baby a great educational start. Looking your baby square in the eye and singing to them is likened to taking your baby to Harvard.

Parents ask me all the time when I tell them this, "Well what do you sing to your baby?" Well, with all of my children the "Alphabet Song" or "ABC song" is always a hit! It really matters not what you sing to your child, the point is that you sing! I know you may be thinking or even complaining, "But I don't have a great singing voice". Well it does not matter. Sing to your baby anyway, and I promise you they will not complain. Developing intelligent children requires selfless, embarrassment. If you are ashamed to make a fool of yourself, then put this book down now. However, if you do care about giving your child a head start in learning to read, then go into a secluded quiet room (If you afraid of being heard by others) and sing to that baby!

Music trains the subconscious minds of baby's and infants in the same way it trains the adult mind. If you are not familiar with the subconscious mind I will explain it as simply as I can.

The subconscious mind is the mind that is always aware and awake, even when you are not. It is the mind that always remembers everything. Take for instance, a street address to a home you used to live in years ago. You may have thought that you have forgotten the address until someone says it aloud to you. Then you have what Oprah refers to as an "Ah-ha moment". Suddenly you realize that you now suddenly remember the address. Well the truth is, you never forgot the address at all, but rather that it was stored in your subconscious mind, waiting to be retrieved.

In order to have a child that speaks and reads at a young age you must flood their subconscious mind with whatever you desire for them to know. Children have to have something in their subconscious minds to retrieve. This is easily done through music.

As my children were growing up my car was used as the main method of transportation. (Specifically, because my car could fit all the car seats). I used "car rides with mommy" as another opportunity to impress upon their subconscious minds through music. I often play a child's music cd in the car. The cd I choose has traditional children's songs such as, BINGO, Old MacDonald, Itsy, Bitsy Spider, and of course the ABC song. Playing that cd has nothing to do with me, and everything to do with my children.

Countless times my husband, sister, or friend will ride with the babies and I and say, "Do you really listen to this?" I simply reply, "They do" (referring to the children). Children are sponges, soaking up everything around them both consciously and subconsciously.

Your role as a teacher/parent is to make sure the material your child or children are exposed to is reflective of the goals you have set for them. Listening to your favorite Hip-Hop, Rap, R&B, Country, Funk, Pop or Jazz song is not as important as the goal you have set for your child. The reality is that any and everything you play for them is being absorbed in their subconscious mind.

I'm sure you have left the car with a tune from a particular song you just listened to completely stuck in your head. Your children are no different. The question is would you rather the Alphabet song be stuck in their heads or the latest Beyoncé single. No offense to Beyoncé or any other pop star or song, but in comparison it is easy to see that the Alphabet Song is far more likely to help give your child a phonemic foundation rather than the latest song to chart the billboards.

Using music to train the subconscious mind of your child does not mean you cannot listen to your personal favorites. It simply means that you are aware of what you allow your child to listen to and what you present to them. For example, one mainstream song played pretty often in our home is "Happy" by Pharell Williams. One morning Pharell performed the song live on Good Morning America and my mother recorded the show. She replayed the recording whenever my children were with her. Of course she sang and danced along with the kids to the song. Engaging children through music is critical. It gave my children a frame of reference when it came time to teach emotions. For example, around that same time my oldest daughter Love was about 15 months old. She would hear her 5-month-old brother crying and say, " Charles no happy". At first I was shocked that she was able to articulate her feelings, but then I began to notice through her vocabulary she was making connections between the word "happy" from the song, the feeling of being happy, and the feeling of not being happy. Through that one song I was able to teach emotion, compare and contrast, cause and effect, and vocabulary development.

Subconscious training through music is all about giving your child a foundation from which they can make connections. This book will show you that when it comes to babies, toddlers, and children, "Everything is everything". Using music as a tool to flood and train the subconscious mind of your child is a great first step.

# CHAPTER FIVE

## *PROGRAMING*

When I was a new mother, I listened to what others had to say about what to do with my baby. I listened intently to their advice, until I came to the realization that although well intentioned, most people are idiots. I found that the people, who have the most advice to give you about what to do with your own child, do not even have children. I remember being at church with my first born, and a woman out of the blue told me to never allow my baby to watch TV. Apparently she read or heard somewhere about television damaging the eyes of babies. I took her advice to heart and when I got home I became obsessed with making sure my little one never caught a glimpse of television. That same night I was given this amazing advice from a church member, my husband was playing with our daughter and the baby channel was on the television in the background. In a "matter of fact" tone I expressed that, "you know today in church so and so said that T.V. is bad for babies. My husband looked at me and said, "Well you do know that so and so doesn't have any kids. I felt like a fool. He was right. I was taking the opinion of a person who does not have any kids as fact without even considering the source of information she presented.

This particular chapter lends itself towards the more open-minded parent. There are some things that you will agree with in this chapter and some things that you may not agree with at all. All that I ask is that you read this chapter knowing full well the education and personal mothering experience it was derived from. The nature of what will be shared in this chapter might go against everything you have been told about television, smart phone applications, and computer programs. I caution that progressive thinkers, who are fully committed to reaching their children by using what works, should only read this chapter. To quote the late great Jonnie Coleman, "It works if you work it!"

Television programing can be done right, and in some cases can be done horribly wrong. We all are familiar with instances when television is used to babysit the child. Now those instances of course are when television is horribly wrong. However, contrary to some belief television programing can effectively be used to supplement instruction. I will give you a scenario where television was used both effectively and ineffectively.

When I was about two or three years old. My mother worked outside the home and my father took care of me during the day. Now by taking care of me I mean that he recorded a full VHS tape full of Sesame Street episodes, and played that tape until the program aired on Television, in which case my dad would then come into the playroom, turn off the tape and let the daily Sesame Street program air for an hour. Now I know you are thinking, "My lord what an awful father." Say what you will, but the truth of the matter is, although flawed on many levels in his childcare approach, my dad couldn't have chosen a better program to have me watch day in and day out. By the age of three without any direct instruction, I knew all my numbers, letter, and colors. One error in his use of programing was that he left the room. Not watching with the child causes the television to watch the child instead of the child watching the program. Television shown without a parent or adult guiding and provoking thinking and learning is of very little benefit and can cause a lack of creativity in the child. The hours of Sesame Street caused me to learn the information presented in the program, however I was unable to form creative thought independent of the program. The truth is that television, (especially if used in complete isolation) does not foster or develop independent or creative thought in any way. Because of this, I do not recommend that television be used in isolation, nor independently with babies, toddlers, or children. Doing so is of very little educational benefit of the child.

I fully understand that as parents we do at times rely on television to "help out" every now and then. For example, you may need or want to cook dinner, so you sit little Johnny in front of the television for a few minutes. There is nothing wrong with this as it is done sparingly and for only a few minutes. The key question (which is in many ways related to the chapter on music) is, "What is the child viewing on the television?" The point is to make sure the programing that the child is watching is of some educational benefit. There are several networks that that take pride in providing relevant, educational programing for babies, toddlers, and children.

Believing that television is never beneficial to children is error thinking. The truth is that there are several ways to gain benefit from television programing. Television reaches the visual learner, which is the learning style of many children. Just as adults have their favorite programs, children do as well. The key is to expose them to programs that present educational content. Make those programs, your child's "Favorite".

One way to enrich the learning experience through programing is to watch the program with the child. Doing this may appear to be a simplistic solution, however the idea is still present within many parents that authentic learning occurs when children are watching programs alone. This is not true. You should sit down with your child. Sit them next to you or on your lap. Put your cell phone or computer down, and watch what they are watching.

While watching the program with your child be sure to highlight educational aspects of the program. By highlighting I mean take one aspect of the program and talk about it with your child. Encourage him or her to talk about it with you. For example, if the program is counting, count aloud with your child. If the program has a letter or color that you want your child to know, talk about that color, letter, or concept with your child. Commit yourself to being an active participant in your child's programing experience. If you choose to use television then make it interactive for the child. Make sure you dance and sing along with the characters. Remember that the use of television programing can be done effectively to enrich your child's learning.

Another form of programing that has been given a bad

reputation are applications or "apps" on cell phones and tablets. Children are interested in things that we as adults are interested. I use my cell phone quite often so naturally my daughter developed an interest in my phone. I wanted to teach her sign language so I downloaded a sign language app to reinforce the words and signs I taught her. The application would simply have an animated baby say and sign common words, such as tree, hi, baby, all done etc. Without prompting my daughter would repeat the words from the baby on the application with impeccable diction and accuracy.

Using cell phone and tablet applications to increase the learning experience of your child is similar to the guidelines for television use; Only in moderation for a few minutes at a time and the adult must be an active participant. Your child should not manipulate a phone, tablet or computer alone or unassisted for prolonged periods of time. Using cell phones, computers, and tablets alone will invariably lead to antisocialism and stifled creative thinking. Both antisocialism and stifled creative thinking are counter productive to the goal of giving your child an educational advantage. The best way to have your child gain some benefit from cell phones, computers, and tablet use is to be an active participant with your child as they use those devices. Remember it is all about how you use the programing that makes the difference.

# CHAPTER SIX

## *REPETITION*

Have you heard the old adage? "Repetition is the mother of learning". Well as antiquated as the belief may be in the mind of progressive authorities in the education community; that saying is true! No matter the subject if you repeatedly immerse a student in that particular subject, then they will learn that particular subject. The main issue is what are you repeatedly saying, and what are you repeatedly doing with your little one? Are you repeatedly demonstrating poor language and communication skills? Are you using baby talk or slang? Are you promoting literacy skills? Are you engaging your child in meaningful conversation? What are you repeating?

Repetition in its simplest form can be incorporated through the use of your routine. For instance, if your goal is to have your child know their letters, then it is only reasonable to expose the child to the alphabet repeatedly. The child could go over the alphabet when they wake up, during breakfast, while traveling in the car, and again before bed. If you follow the simple model written in the previous sentences; then it will be four times in one day where you have explicitly and repeatedly exposed your child to the alphabet. Doing continually and repeatedly until the child knows all 26 letters should only take a matter of weeks provided you are consistent with the repetition schedule you choose.

As we move through this chapter on repetition, I am aware that you may be thinking, " How in the world am I supposed to get my child to repeat after me when they cannot even talk. Well that is the thing about repetition; you are guiding their thinking with or without actual repetition taking place. (The chapter on flashcards will provide a detailed account of how to teach through repetition when the student cannot talk.)

Most children enjoy repetition without being fully aware. Children will request you read the same book to them repeatedly. Children will watch the same program repeatedly. They will sing the same songs repeatedly. They will also play the same games repeatedly. I remember one time my sister in law shipped my son a birthday gift. The gift was a talking bear that sang "Happy Birthday". As expected my daughter (10 months older than my son) had to have that bear! She figured out how to work the paw and make the bear sing. She then began to play and manipulate the bear. I just sat there and watched her play. She continually turned the singing bear on and off. She danced to the rhythm and tried to sing along. She literally played with that bear for seven whole minutes. She played with the singing bear so long I thought the batteries would die. When children are interested in any one thing they will play with it repeatedly.

My son (10 months younger than my daughter) went through a phase where he loved to see and make things spin. He would turn toy cars upside down and spin the wheels for what seemed like hours. My son would take tops, and bottles, and practically anything he could and spin them on the floor. Spinning things fascinated him and kept his attention for minutes (In baby/infant time that is a long time ☺). Repetition is in many ways the language of children.

I'm sure you have many stories or could think of a time when your little one repeatedly did something or played with something. At that time I am sure you wondered would they ever get tired of the particular thing they were playing with. Well as a parent or guardian it is our job to present children with these things you don't mind the child "over dosing" on. For example, who would ever say, I wish my child would stop counting backwards, or saying their alphabet, or identifying shapes and colors. Not many parents would find that sort of repetition too much, right.

Repetition in many ways can provide the framework for critical thinking skills such as inferring. You may be thinking, "Well my child can barely speak, how in the world do you think they can infer". Well let me share with you that repetition lays the groundwork for inference by providing a foundation.

My daughter was persistent about reading the book "Jazz Baby" or rather me reading that book to her everyday! So for about a week I read the book "Jazz Baby" to her and my son. Now "Jazz Baby" not only rhymes but it also has a distinct rhythm and flow. I continually read this same book to her (she was 20 months at the time) and by the end of the week she could do the most remarkable thing. On each page I could leave off the last word, and she would fill in the missing word. By the use of repetition my one year old was able to not only correctly infer what word would come next in the story, but also she was able to exercise her memory in doing so as well as identify rhyming words in the book.

Repetition is not a lost art. It can easily be done to foster early literacy development. Take time each day to teach your child something beneficial …………repeatedly.

# THE CONSCIOUS MIND OF YOUR CHILD

# CHAPTER SEVEN

## *DIRECT INSTRUCTION*

The previous chapters explained and focused on subconscious training or as I refer to "what is going on in the background. Well, the next few chapters will delve into conscious training; meaning what children are learning in the foreground. Conscious training is explicit instruction, whether it is one on one or in a group setting. Conscious training is actually teaching your child what you want him or her to know or learn. This can be done easily through the instructional tools of flashcards, books, and games. The proceeding chapters will share effective techniques to provide direct instruction.

Flashcards

Flashcards just like repetition have been categorized as an antiquated way of learning. However, I have found flashcards to be an extremely engaging outlet for young students. Traditionally flashcards have been used in a boring quizzing fashion, which only allows the participation of the facilitator as a bit of a lecturer. The way that I am suggesting that they be used, involves the child as an active participant in the process.

The first step to using flashcards as a tool is to actually buy or make flashcards. Many dollar stores or school supplies stores will carry alphabet flash cards, and they can easily be printed from various sources online. The key is to be sure that the cards you choose to purchase have a picture that coincides with the correct sound that that letter makes. For example, I once purchased flash cards from a dollar store. When I began working with my daughter and these cards, I noticed the letter "E " had a picture with the word "eye". Now, that is very confusing as the letter "E" does not make an "I" sound. The letter "e" makes the "eh" sound. To account for this error I placed a picture of an "egg" over the "eye" and corrected the error aloud when going over the flash cards.

Now that you have alphabet flash cards it is time to put them to great use. The first thing I did with my daughter when she was younger was to sit her in my lap. Sitting her in my lap not only provided the security of my closeness but also gave great focus to the lesson at hand. If you allow the child to float all around the room, then they will easily be distracted by everything besides the flashcards. When using the cards, also make sure that all television programing, computers, and cell phones, are powered off. Flash card time is direct instruction; therefore the main focus should always be placed on the time spent between you and the child. You and your child should be uninterrupted.

Once the baby or child is on your lap with no distractions. You are ready to begin. Start by first telling the child what you intend to teach or go over. This sets the purpose and focus of the lesson. You'll be able to help the child to express when he/she wants to use the flashcards again. Simply say, " Today we are going to go over the letters in the alphabet and their sounds. " If the child appears disinterested, then pick up the flash card and say "ooh", "look at this", and "wow". Children will get as excited about any subject based on your level of excitement. Therefore, it is very important that you act extremely excited about the cards and the child will follow suit in your level of excitement.

Next, you will need to take the child's hand. Doing this allows the child to physically participate in the instruction. Simply grab the hand of the child and touch the card, as you say the letter. Then the word, and finally the sound. So for example, say "A" (then point to the letter "A"). Next say "apple" (then point to the apple) and lastly say the sound that the letter "A" makes. Then have your child or baby repeat after you. Now in the instance that your child/baby cannot repeat after you, then it becomes your job to repeat for them. Modeling repetition is of great benefit to the child as it exposes the child to the letter, word, and sound, not once but twice. Do not think for one second that repeating for the child is pointless; remember that the child's subconscious mind is always at work. Any exposure to phonemic awareness is good exposure. Repeat each letter, word, and sound at least once everyday. Incorporate flashcards into your daily routine, whether it is at night, in the morning, or during a meal. After about a full week of consistent use of flashcards, (if the child can talk then praise them profusely at any letters they are able to identify independently. This encouragement and praise tells the child not only that they are doing a good job. But also that learning is something that you as a parent or guardian care about.

Remember to always have the child touch the card as you say the word, sound, and letter. Doing this makes flashcards more of a physical activity and engages the active learner. . This is especially true for the child who can hardly sit still) Flashcards are not outdated and are extremely beneficial to the phonemic awareness of your little learner. Just follow the detailed instructions provided concerning flashcards, and know that you are using them in the most effective way. Your young child will reap the benefits and eventually learn to read.

# CHAPTER EIGHT

## *BOOKS*

Any educator worth their salt will tell you the great and grand importance of reading books to your child. Many times I am asked, "What should I read to my child?" That common question can be summed up in one word. "Everything". Read everything to your child. Read the words on their clothes and shoes. Read the menus when you go out to eat. Read the street signs. Read the words on boxes and toys. And most importantly read books, no matter the length, size or level. Read books to your child both intentionally and often. The child needs to hear you read. The toddler needs to hear you read. The baby needs to hear you read. Reading to your child not only models for him/her the rhythm and pace of fluent reading, but it also exposes him/her to vocabulary that is not typically used on a daily basis.

Vocabulary development is very important to early literacy. According to a study done by the center for education at Rice University, (2003), "Children from families on welfare hear about 616 words per hour, while those from working class families hear about 1,251 words per hour, and those from professional families hear roughly 2, 153 words per hour." No matter where you and your family fall on the income spectrum, the one thing that can be done to gain and maintain language exposure is to read to your child. If your house is not blessed to have an overabundance of books, then simply use what you do have. Read the labels on the cereal box to the child. Read the nutrition labels. Read aloud the text messages and emails, you give and receive. Read the junk mail that includes the sales papers. Read everything. Reading everything provides an excellent foundation for early literacy skills.

# CHAPTER NINE

## *QUESTIONING*

I wouldn't suggest giving your child a formal quiz. However, it is important to gage what your child is learning. You need to know which concepts he/she has not yet grasped, and those subjects that you should work on. This can effectively be done through questioning.

There are two types of questions. Open ended and closed. An open-ended question allows for multiple answers, and really gives the child a chance to demonstrate his/her understanding on a topic. Although your child or baby may only be able to say a few words, it is important to lend yourself towards open-ended questions with your little one. Ask him/her to tell you how something works, or tell you what letter comes next in a word. Allow your child to give an answer that is constructed from his/her own thinking.

Furthermore, asking open-ended questions will also give you an opportunity to model responses to questions. For example, when your child begins to give you one word requests and one word answers to questions, you can encourage them to speak to you in sentences. I wanted my daughter to know her name, so I would ask her, "What is your name?" (A simple question a stranger or friend might ask her) she would respond, "Wove" I would have her repeat after me and say, "My name is Love Bradley". My daughter and I would go over this routine about twice or more each day. Then, one time we were riding in the car and out of nowhere with perfect diction and rhythm, she said, " My name is Love Bradley". I almost had to pull over the car. I was shocked she spoke in a complete sentence, unprompted, and without repeating. This was a major accomplishment and it started from my asking her open-ended questions. Asking open-ended questions is an effective way to get your child to talk to you and encourage him/her to voice their feelings and emotions. Examples of a few open-ended questions are, "What do you want?" "Tell me about what you are eating?" "Why are you crying?" All of these questions require a constructed response from the child and foster thinking. Your child may even speak to you in a sentence at the age of one or two years old!

On the other hand asking closed ended questions can lead to stifled thought and lack of critical thinking. Closed ended questions are questions that require a yes or no answer. Those questions don't require the child to actually think or say many words. Examples of those questions are, "Do you want to eat?" "Do you like this toy? ""Are you ready to go? " "Do you have to go potty?" The problem with close-ended questions is that they generally elicit an incorrect response from toddlers.

There are two different types of toddlers. There are toddlers that respond, "yes" to everything. And there are toddlers that respond "no" to everything. For this reason I do not recommended that you use close-ended questions to you're your toddlers understanding. There was one time in particular when my daughter impressed my husband by responding "No" when he asked her, "Do you want a sandwich? He said, "Look she really knows what she wants." I said, "No, she actually just likes saying "No"." "Watch this. I asked her if she wanted some candy, if she wanted a treat, and if she wanted her all time favorite, juice. All questions were of course answered by my then 15 month old, "No". She invariably did not know what I was asking.

She has an older cousin and he was a "yes" man. I would play with him just to hear him say "yes" I would ask him, do you want a sandwich? "Yes", Do you want a piece of candy?" yes" do you want to go outside? "Yes", do you want some broccoli? "Yes" Do you want a spanking? "Yes". Go on and laugh. I also thought it to be pretty funny that a two year old would want a spanking.

Be sure that when getting information from the child that the questions you ask them are varied. Sometimes closed questions are good for obtaining information that you want to know quickly. However, when the child is young, closed questions cannot be relied upon to gain or gage the child's understanding.

# _Moving Forward_

# CHAPTER TEN

## *LETTER MASTERY AND BLENDS*

A good determination of letter mastery for children, involve two separate items. Letter recognition in and out of sequential order, and letter renunciation. Those two items determine letter mastery and in a sense should be the start and basis for moving forward with teaching your child to read.

First, begin by making sure your child has mastered the recognition of letters. This can be done in a variety of ways. You can use the methods used in the previous chapters to encourage your child to master his/her letters. With my child the most effective method of teaching her the letters of the alphabet was the use of flashcards. I began with going over the letters and using the repetition method. Where I had her to repeat the letters after me. I began to reinforce letter repetition through a variety of books. There are several children's books that teach letters. Another way that I reinforced our lessons on letters was the use of television programing and cell phone applications. When I taught my daughter her letters I used every avenue to expose her to letters in and out of context.

Letter renunciation I found happened as a subset of direct instruction. What I mean by that is, she began to sing the alphabet song without it being intentionally, and explicitly taught. After hearing the alphabet song, through singing it at home and in the car. She was also exposed to flash cards and cd's therefore, Love was able to more or less simply pick up on the song. One night I was making spaghetti and as I stood at the counter chopping onions, I heard my daughter who was sitting in her high chair, singing away. I immediately stopped chopping and listened to what she was singing. She began "a, b, c, d, e, f, g, h, I, j, k, lmno (all said together), p, q, r, s, t, u, v, w, x, y, z now I know my abc next time wont you (something inaudible) sing with me." I was shocked, because again the alphabet song was not something explicitly taught to her. However, she picked up on the song through what I call background mediums.

There was a video that went viral with a father and his 16-month-old baby. The father had large cards scattered on the floor with words printed on them. The words were simple sight words, "tree, bird, flower, etc." The father would say, "Hand me the tree". Next the baby would waddle around the floor until he found the word tree and then hand the card to his father. That video is incredibly adorable and the father was highly praised for teaching his son to "read". However, his son was not in fact reading at all. The baby had memorized the look of the words and was able to identify them. I see a bit of a flaw in this technique, which is that the child is learning by recognizing symbols and not actually reading phonetically. Think about what happens when the child forgets a word. They will not be able to sound it out because they do not know the letter sounds. I think many people may be mistaking this for reading.

This method is only beneficial with sight words that don't adhere to English rules. I see that video as a positive video and I applaud the parent for valuing education. However, eventually the child will have to start over by learning to recognize the letters and be able to identify the letter's sound. Thus allowing him to learn how to group these letters together to create functioning words. This program is flawed because if you were to ask the child to point to the letter A and give the associated sound they wouldn't be able to do this. That means in actuality the child cannot read, but rather can identify a symbol much like they would a shape such as a circle.

The more effective way of teaching reading is to do what I proposed which is to teach the child to first identify letters. Once mastery of letters is gained then you can move forward teaching the phoneme or "letter sound".

Sounds

Teaching letter sounds to small children can be done in two ways. Letter sounds can be taught along with letter recognition or letter sounds can be taught in isolation. I taught my children their letter sounds while teaching them their letters through flash cards and song. The absolute best song that helps children remember their letter sounds comes from a leapfrog video called, "The Letter Factory". In the video Tad (a frog) is given a tour of the letter factory by Professor Quigley (a mouse) and Tad is taught each letter and sound. The same tune is sang throughout the video that goes, "The A says "AHH", "The A says "AHH", every letter makes a sound the A says "Ahh". It is by far the catchiest song for learning letters and sounds. I played this 30-minute video and within a week or two my daughter knew all of her letter sounds.

There are many different ways you can teach the letter sounds to children. The point is that the child should master letter sounds before moving on to blends and making words. The reason why I share the leapfrog song is because; the last part of the song/rhyme falls on the downbeat, which forces a child to fill in the missing sound. This allows you the parent to gage whether the child actually knows the letter sound in a fun and informal way. My children absolutely loved singing the song and the call and response required in completing the task.

There are several reasons that mastery of letter sounds is important. Mastery of letter sounds is in essence the basis for reading. It gives the child a firm foundation. Imagine your little child with a book in hand completely frustrated at not being able to read a particular word in the book. You are across the room and can ask them how to spell that word. After the child spells the word, you can then ask them, "Well what sound does the first letter start with? What is the second letter? And so on? Knowing letter sounds can help you as a parent guide the child into sounding out unfamiliar words.

Once your child has fully mastered all of the alphabet and the letter sounds, then you can start blending letters together and working on word families. This can be done in a variety of ways.

You can find or create flash cards, use rhyming games, or even simply use blends you find in text. The important part is that the child knows that when two letters are joined together they make a sound called a blend. Some of the common blends are "st", "ch" ,"sh" ,"ck", and "th". These letters make a unique sound when placed next to one another in a word.

Once your child can read simple words, such as, at, sit, up, or know their letters and their sounds, you will notice a significant increase in his/her confidence. Read with your child as much as you can and work on these skills for mastery.

## CHAPTER ELEVEN

## *ON THE RIGHT TRACK*

Picking up this book and reading it means you are on the right track. Even if you do not agree with the subject matter, you are still on the right track. Having read this book shows that you have a desire for your child to excel at an early age academically. Every piece of information that you grasp for the betterment of your child means that you are invariably on the right track. There is absolutely nothing wrong with wanting the best for your little learner. Just as there are many different ways to peel an orange, there are various ways to teach early literacy skills to your child. There's no one specific way. I have merely shared with you the strategies and techniques that I found successful with the young children that I teach.

You should undoubtedly be your child's first teacher. Therefore, quality time must be spent with your child to gain a quality result. If you feel resistance from your child in wanting to do the activities then you must become creative. For example, I was using my teaching methods with a little boy. He was the most active little boy I ever taught. He wouldn't sit still and was all over the place. I knew I had to become creative in my approach with him because his learning style was so incredibly different from my daughters. I immediately stopped trying to teach him and began "reading" him. In observing his every move, I noticed that he would play with a toy for about two minutes then run clean across the room to another toy. He would do this "play and run" game continually. I knew immediately that I needed to incorporate this game into his learning, so I did just that. We would play a letter game with flashcards, then countdown from 10 to 1 and literally run to the other side of the room to play another game. I was able to get through to him, because I was able to reach him at his level.

As a mother, knowing and recognizing the learning style of your child is very easy because you do actually know your child better than anyone else. Take pride in knowing your little one. From their likes and dislikes, you know what best suits their learning style. At a very early age (about 12-15 months) my oldest daughter was enamored with my husband. She would sit face to face on him and he would hum and she would imitate him. This went on for about a week and he began to say words and she would repeat them. I asked him to take it a step further and have her learn facial features, and sure enough she was able to point out several facial features by the weeks end.

Although I consider myself a master teacher, it was evident that for some reason my daughter was learning better from my husband. Subsequently, I made a point to tell him to both teach and reinforce the things I wanted her to learn. In addition to teaching her facial features, my husband also helped to teach my daughter to count to ten, simple words, and lots of other things. It is important to use your village to help your child learn. Even if you feel that you do not have a big village, use whom you have. For instance, if you send your child with a friend or godparent for the day, feel free to tell them what you would like them to go over with the child. One time my daughter was to spend the day with her god mother Krystal, I told her godmother that we were working on saying "thank you". I asked Krystal to use the sign for "thank you" to encourage my daughter to say that phrase. In no time I noticed from that day my oldest daughter spent with her godmother that she was correctly and consistently saying "thank you!".

Use whatever village you have. My father bought a "Star Wars" color book from a book fair and used it to teach my daughter her colors. Teachers are EVERYWHERE; you just have to be wiling to ask for the help.

## Final Thought

Reading is a necessary and inevitable life skill. Teaching children reading skills early will undoubtedly set the stage for early success in academic arenas. As you read this book I know that some of the suggested methods may have resonated with you. Those methods will help you to help your child become an early reader. If you feel like you have tried everything to get your little one to learn, do not worry. Your efforts are not in vain. Your child is absorbing more than he or she is willing to tell you. Stay consistent with whatever methods you choose, and know that in the end the extra effort you made will benefit the child both now and in the future. Continue to talk with your child, even when you question if they are listening. They are listening, so be mindful of what you say. Always be encouraging and always be committed to the best education for them. Rest assured knowing that as you are reading this book, you are on the right track!

# ABOUT THE AUTHOR

Naomi H. Bradley is an extraordinary early childhood and adult educator. She received her Bachelors degree from Kennesaw State University, and Masters degree from Valdosta State University in Middle Grades Math and Science. She founded Love Bradley Academy; a non-profit organization committed to the early literacy and math skills for toddlers and children. Naomi Bradley currently teaches adult education classes at Georgia Piedmont Technical College. She lives in Ellenwood GA with her husband Walter, and three children, Love, Charles, and Faith. Videos of Love reading can be found on Facebook at www.facebook.com/naomi.m.hill

Made in the USA
Charleston, SC
25 March 2015